Animals from Head to Tail

# ALLIGATORS FROM HEAD TO TAIL

By Emmett Martin

**Please visit our website, www.garethstevens.com. For a free color catalog of all our high-quality books, call toll free 1-800-542-2595 or fax 1-877-542-2596.**

**Library of Congress Cataloging-in-Publication Data**

Names: Martin, Emmett, author.
Title: Alligators from head to tail / Emmett Martin.
Description: New York : Gareth Stevens Publishing, [2021] | Series: Animals from head to tail | Includes index.
Identifiers: LCCN 2019042312 | ISBN 9781538255247 (library binding) | ISBN 9781538255223 (paperback) | ISBN 9781538255230 (6 pack)| ISBN 9781538255254 (ebook)
Subjects: LCSH: Alligators–Juvenile literature.
Classification: LCC QL666.C925 M3765 2021 | DDC 597.98/4–dc23
LC record available at https://lccn.loc.gov/2019042312

First Edition

Published in 2021 by
**Gareth Stevens Publishing**
111 East 14th Street, Suite 349
New York, NY 10003



Editor: Therese Shea
Designer: Laura Bowen

Photo credits: Cover, p. 1 Tier Und Naturfotografie J und C Sohns/Photolibrary/Getty Images Plus/Getty Images; pp. 5, 9, 24 (snout) Arto Hakola/Shutterstock.com; p. 7 Lars Schmidt-Eisenlohr/Shutterstock.com; p. 11 SunflowerMomma/Shutterstock.com; p. 13 Darrell Gulin/The Image Bank/Getty Images Plus/Getty Images; p. 15 benedek/iStock/Getty Images Plus/Getty Images; p. 17 chloe7992/Shutterstock.com; p. 19 John Cawthron/Shutterstock.com; pp. 21, 24 (nest) Howcheng/Wikimedia Commons; p. 23 DimaSid/Shutterstock.com.



Printed in the United States of America



CPSIA compliance information: Batch #CS20GS: For further information contact Gareth Stevens, New York, New York at 1-800-542-2595.

# Contents

Alligators are reptiles!

They have thick skin.

They have a long nose.
It's called a snout.
It's round at the end.

They live near water.
They like rivers and lakes.

Alligators swim a lot.
Their eyes stick out!

They have a strong tail.

They have short legs.
They walk and run.

They eat meat.
They eat lots of fish!

They make nests.

They lay eggs.
Babies come out!

# Words to Know

nest

snout

# Index